NO GREATER LOVE

The Martyrdom *of the* Ulma Family

Jean Olwen Maynard

All booklets are published thanks to the generosity of the supporters of the Catholic Truth Society

All rights reserved. First published 2023 by The Incorporated Catholic Truth Society, 42-46 Harleyford Road, London SE11 5AY. Tel: 020 7640 0042. www.ctsbooks.org. © 2023 The Incorporated Catholic Truth Society.

ISBN 978 1 78469 760 0

Contents

Wiktoria and Józef Ulma

A Family of No Importance

This is the story of a family – a mother and father, and their seven children all very small and one not yet born – who were of no importance in the eyes of the world. They lived their lives in an underdeveloped backwater of Central Europe, in a period of history when ideologies of hatred gained such widespread acceptance as to be considered normal and legitimate. Under the power of those ideologies countless numbers of people made choices which led them into horrifying depths of evil and brought suffering and death to millions of others.

It's very difficult for us to enter imaginatively into the atmosphere of those times. Although they weren't so long ago, in many ways they already seem totally alien. It's all too easy for us to perch smugly on the moral high ground, saying to ourselves, *"We'd* never do that." But perhaps we would. Or perhaps at least we'd go along with it. There, but for the grace of God…

Even if we can't fully grasp the why and the how of it all, we do need to know about what happened. A firm consensus against permitting those terrible crimes to be forgotten and swept under the carpet provides a safeguard against letting them happen again. It is also a way of showing respect, something we owe to the dead.

The Ulmas loved each other and lived happily together – something not all families are able to achieve. Other than that, their material circumstances didn't allow much scope for noteworthy achievement. In an act of rare heroism, they put themselves at risk to save two other families, but their efforts ended in total failure with everyone killed.

Their story is nevertheless a bright light shining in the darkness. Through it God is saying to us something the world cannot hear. That each and every human person is infinitely precious in his sight. And that he designed us to be born and grow up in families, profoundly bound up with one another so that even in our fallen condition we might come to understand something of how truly precious each person is. The Ulmas didn't have advanced degrees in theology, but they absolutely knew all this in their hearts. This is why the Church recognises them as having given their lives for the sake of the Gospel: as martyrs, slain by the forces of evil out of hatred for the Faith.

Poland: Land of Opportunity

Poland in the Middle Ages covered a huge area. At one period it was the largest country in Europe. Although it had plenty of land, there were not enough people to work it, and it was also relatively underdeveloped, so it was government policy to encourage and welcome immigrants. Large numbers of German-speaking people were drawn into the Polish lands, including large numbers of Jews. None of them spoke what we would recognise as standard German: the different groups spoke a wide range of dialects, and the Jews had their own dialect known as Yiddish, which was written using the Hebrew alphabet. Many of the immigrants brought valuable skills and know-how, but such was the demand for labour that everyone was welcome even if all they could bring was a strong pair of hands.

The Jews were particularly happy about moving to Poland. They had been violently expelled from England and France, and almost everywhere else in Western Europe they were being subjected to discriminatory legislation if not outright persecution – constantly mounting pressures which would often culminate in further wholesale expulsions or coercive conversions to Christianity. Poland, by contrast, was religiously pluralistic and offered a very wide freedom of belief and practice to all kinds of religious groups. Immigrant communities could keep their own language and culture, and even maintain a degree of self-governance – options which the Jews eagerly adopted. Poland was the only country in Europe where Jewish farmers were entitled to own the land they tilled. From the sixteenth century, the Jews of Poland experienced a golden age in which Jewish culture and rabbinic learning flourished wonderfully.

Partition of Poland

During the eighteenth century, Poland was wiped off the map when the Polish lands and their people were partitioned between the neighbouring states of Austria, Prussia (later to become the core of a united Germany) and Russia. Southern Poland became a province of Austria and was renamed Galicia. The western half of Galicia was inhabited predominantly by Polish-speaking Catholics and the eastern half by Ukrainian-speaking Orthodox or Greek Catholics. About ten per cent of its population was Jewish, and it was among the Jews of Galicia that there arose the Hasidic movement of spiritual renewal within Judaism which is still important today.

Galicia became a byword for underdevelopment and desperate poverty. As in Ireland before the Potato Famine, the region had a very high birth rate, and because family plots in each generation had to be subdivided among all the sons, farms kept getting smaller and smaller. Moreover, because the farming techniques had hardly changed since the Middle Ages, they produced far less food than they could have done with better know-how. Galicia was a place people dreamed of getting out of, and towards the end of the nineteenth century between two and three million Galicians did get out – some emigrating to other parts of the Austrian Empire, and many to the USA, Canada or Brazil. The Polish Galicians had begun the trend, but the Jewish and Ukrainian Galicians quickly joined it, making new lives for themselves elsewhere. Despite the high emigration rate the population density in Galicia remained high.

Poland restored

Successive Polish uprisings during the nineteenth century had failed to throw off the foreign yoke and been brutally repressed. During the First World War however all the major belligerents began issuing pledges (mostly vague) for the restoration of Poland, as a way of recruiting Poles to fight on their side. The end of the war in 1918 saw the collapse of the German and Austrian Empires, while the Russian Empire had been taken over by the Communists and was in a state of civil war. This left a vacuum of power in Central Europe in which Poland could re-emerge as a sovereign state. An international consensus was coming together in favour of the dismantling of the old empires and allowing previously subjugated peoples to form themselves into self-governing nations, but the reality on the ground was that the different ethnic groups were mixed up and scattered all over the place.

An independent Poland would almost certainly have been restored by agreement between the Allied Powers, but the Poles fought fiercely to recover all the areas inhabited by Polish speakers or which had historically belonged to Poland. In consequence, the interwar Polish Republic was considerably larger than it might otherwise have been, with boundaries that were bitterly disputed by its neighbours, and a third of its population non-Polish. It had substantial Ukrainian, Belarusian, Czech, Lithuanian, German and Jewish minorities, all of which had their own mother tongues and were keen to preserve their distinctive identity and bring up their children in their own cultural traditions. The majority Polish community would in pre-modern times have been thoroughly laid back about that, but the first half of the twentieth century was far too dominated by ethnonationalist ideologies. Moreover, although adversity can make people kinder and more sympathetic towards others, it often has the opposite effect, especially when the entire society they identify with has spent generations being pushed around and humiliated. It is also often the case that in such situations the most angry and aggressive rise to the top and steer developments, lashing out at anyone who is "different". Accordingly, the Poles were inclined to view their country's ethnic minorities with hostility and suspicion.

In practice, each minority was treated differently. The Germans bitterly resented ending up in Poland and were constantly complaining, though they were not, in fact, noticeably ill-treated. The Ukrainians in eastern Galicia, and in Volhynia which lay even farther east and had only a tiny percentage of Poles in its population, fared far worse. They had very much wanted to have a country of their own rather than being split between Poland and the Soviet Union. Poland had promised them a fair degree of regional autonomy, but the promise wasn't kept, and they felt that they were treated as second-class citizens. During the 1930s, Ukrainian nationalists began resorting to terrorism and sabotage, and the Polish state responded with harsh reprisals which alienated the Ukrainians more than ever. During the years of partition, the Roman Catholic Church had provided the Polish people with a safe space for expressing and nurturing their Polishness, and religious allegiance had come to serve as a crude identifier of nationality. Accordingly, the repressive measures against the Ukrainians included religious persecution of Orthodox Christians and efforts at forcibly converting them to Roman Catholicism in order to make them "properly Polish".

The rise of anti-Semitism

Unlike the other minorities, the Jews were broadly supportive of the Polish Republic, but remained culturally separated. They maintained their own Yiddish-language educational system, literature and newspapers, theatres, film industry, and sports clubs – all vibrant and remarkably successful – as well as their own political parties. A very high proportion couldn't understand Polish. None of that went down well with the increasingly twitchy Polish nationalists. Moreover, the Jews, like the Ukrainians, belonged to a stateless nation and as such offered a soft target. Within Polish Catholic society there emerged a growing tide of anti-Semitism, and as the global Great Depression set in, the Jews were increasingly blamed for the spread of unemployment and economic hardship. In fairness to the Poles, this was part of a global trend: anti-Semitic attitudes and organised anti-Semitic movements were very much on the rise at this time throughout most of Europe and North America. Even in the UK, attitudes towards Jews which would nowadays be considered totally unacceptable were firmly within the spectrum of normal public discourse.

It didn't help that interwar Poland was struggling with quite a serious overpopulation problem, in the sense that it had too many people to be able to offer a decent living from traditional agriculture and was insufficiently industrialised to provide alternative options. Józef

Piłsudski, hero of the fight for independence and head of state from 1926, when the authoritarian and militaristic Sanacja movement seized power in a coup, managed to keep a lid on things. Although he ruled as a quasi-dictator, he enjoyed quite broad popular support and was not anti-Semitic. After his death in 1935 the Sanacja regime tried to play the anti-Semitism card, thinking it would be a vote-catcher, and the position of the Jews began to look quite worrying. It became official policy to encourage Jews to emigrate, partly because many of them saw that as quite a positive solution. In pursuance of this end, the government co-operated eagerly with the Zionist movement, which was actively seeking to relocate Jews to Palestine. Many would have preferred to go to America, but since the First World War the US had brought in immigration restrictions – as indeed had the UK – making that a lot more difficult than before.

"We are spiritually Semites"

Historically it had been commonplace for Catholics to take a negative view of the Jews. During the first few decades of the twentieth century the Catholic Church underwent severe persecution in many parts of the world – the Soviet Union and Mexico, and in Spain following the outbreak of the Civil War – at the hands of left-wing political forces. International opinion responded with indifference, insisting that the reports were untrue or exaggerated, or that the Catholics deserved it. When the Jews began asking Catholic leaders to speak up for them, their initial reaction was to ask why they should, since the Jews had never spoken up for the Catholics. The Church rightly took a stand against violent and viciously anti-religious forms of socialism, which were a real threat to human well-being, and against amoral capitalism which put profits before people. Sadly, however, during this period when assumptions that the Jews were somehow specially responsible for one or other of these developments, or (illogically) both, were finding widespread acceptance, Catholic leaders were also taken in by them.

Nevertheless, towards the end of the 1930s the realisation dawned that the forces of anti-Semitism – above all in Germany – had gone too far. Speaking to pilgrims visiting Rome who had presented him with a missal, Pope Pius XI drew attention to the part in the Eucharistic Prayer referring to "the sacrifice of Abraham, our father in faith" and unexpectedly departed from his written text to issue a strong statement condemning anti-Semitism. "Through Christ and in Christ we are Abraham's descendants. No, it is not possible for Christians to take part in anti-Semitism... We are spiritually Semites."

Markowa

The village of Markowa lay in Galicia, in a very hilly and forested area of Poland which even today is relatively underdeveloped and less well-off than the rest of the country. In terms of the administrative divisions which prevailed in interwar Poland, this area formed the western half of a considerably larger province of which Lwów (now Lviv in Ukraine) – about a hundred miles to the east – was the provincial capital. The population of this interwar province was ethnically quite mixed, but by and large the western half was predominantly Polish. In the eastern half, the rural population was quite strongly Ukrainian, but the city of Lwów was essentially Polish. Slightly over half of the city residents were Polish, a third, Jewish, and only about a sixth, Ukrainian. Lwów was Poland's third largest city, and in terms of cultural importance, second only to Warsaw.

Markowa was founded in the fourteenth century by the Pileckis, the noble family which at that time owned the nearby town of Łańcut and lived in the castle that dominated the town. The Pileckis brought ethnic German farming families to settle in the new village. The first inhabitants still identified as German and spoke German among themselves, so they named the village Markhof, but over the centuries their descendants became completely polonised, and once they'd completely forgotten the German language the name was corrupted to Markowa. As of the late-1930s Markowa was one of the largest villages in Poland, with nearly 4,500 inhabitants. About seventy per cent still bore German surnames, but they'd come to think of themselves simply as Polish. Overwhelmingly they were Catholics, and peasant farmers. Considering themselves peasants didn't mean they were submissive and downtrodden: on the contrary, they saw it as a source of pride. Galicia was a stronghold of the Polish peasant movement, which had its own political party. Pro-democratic and in favour of

land reform, the Peasant Party was an important source of opposition to the Sanacja. The peasant movement was all for modernity and progress – and for education, provided that it wasn't the kind that would suck young people out of the countryside and make them feel ashamed of getting their hands dirty.

In 1932, peasant leaders from Markowa took the lead in setting up a people's university in the village of Gać, near the town of Przeworsk a few miles to the east. It was named the Orkan University after a recently deceased Polish writer who'd specialised in writing novels and short stories about village life. The presence of the Orkan University, and the vibrant, go-ahead attitudes that prevailed in Markowa, proved a magnet, attracting progressive-minded people to settle in and around the

Markowa

locality and contribute their ideas and energy to making good things happen there. Ignacy Solarz, a well-known educator and activist in the peasant movement, who was the most prominent promoter in Poland of the people's universities, resigned from an older one near Kraków which was by now well-established and came to run the Orkan University. Solarz had also been responsible for founding the Union of Rural Youth – popularly known as Wici – in 1928, when a pre-existing peasant youth movement had split over the issue of support for the Sanacja. Under Solarz's guidance, Wici broke away to remain free from political co-option by the regime.

Jews in Markowa

Also in Markowa lived two dozen or so Jewish families – altogether about 120 Jewish individuals. There was one section of the village where seven of the houses strung along the road belonged to Jews, and that part was jokingly known as Kazimierz, after the large and rather splendid Jewish quarter in Kraków. Mostly, however, the Jewish homes were scattered among the Polish ones, not clumped together in any particular area. Interestingly, in the 1921 census, in which most Jews across Poland put their nationality down as Jewish, out of the 126 Markowa villagers who put down their religion as Judaism only five chose to declare themselves Jewish by nationality: all the rest put themselves down as Polish.

They made their living primarily from wholesale trading and shopkeeping, though some of them farmed a bit on the side. Chaim and Estera Goldman, who had a house and shop on the main crossroads from where the roads led off to the various towns round about, naturally did a roaring trade and were among the best-off of the village's Jewish families.

Poles and Jews in Markowa tended to socialise mainly within their own communities, and this naturally fostered a sense of otherness on both sides. The children all attended the village school together, though the Jewish children formed a very small minority, and there is evidence that they were targeted for bullying. They had their own classes outside school hours to learn about Judaism and Jewish culture. On Good Friday it was traditional for the Polish youngsters to make guys, representing Judas, to be beaten, hanged and finally burned, and some of the teenagers thought it was funny to hang up the Judas effigies in front of the Jewish houses. Nevertheless, the village adults seem on the whole to have rubbed along peacefully. Polish and Jewish families who were near neighbours tended to know each other and be on friendly terms. Some of the older Poles strongly disapproved of the stunts with the Judas effigies, but getting teenagers to desist from anti-social behaviour is always an uphill task.

Józef and Wiktoria Ulma

Józef Ulma was born in Markowa on 2nd March 1900. His parents were peasant farmers who owned about seven and a half acres of land and a small wooden house. Markowa was in the Diocese of Przemyśl which – during all the time little Józef was growing up – had an unusually holy and inspirational Bishop: Józef Pelczar, who died in 1924 and has since been canonised. Markowa itself had a particularly zealous parish priest in Fr Władisław Tryczyński who in 1904 persuaded the villagers that it was time to replace their old wooden church with something better. A design was duly commissioned from Stanisław Majerski, a Przemyśl architect whose work was becoming very popular in the diocese. Consecrated in 1910, the new church of St Dorota was in the gothic revival style and looked very impressive. Reflecting the ethnic mix of this part of Poland, Majerski designed a few churches for Orthodox and Greek Catholic Ukrainian parishes, along with about twenty for Roman Catholic Polish ones. He also designed two smart synagogues for Przemyśl: the New Synagogue, and the Tempel Synagogue where – unusually – the services were conducted in Polish.

Józef Ulma took his Catholic faith seriously. As a teenager he joined a diocesan Eucharistic Union, committing to pray and fundraise for the building of more local churches and chapels. He also belonged to the Catholic Youth Association, at the same time as being very active in Wici. Wici was quite left-wing, and the parish priest didn't approve of it, but Józef was quite capable of deciding such matters for himself and took no notice of Father Tryczyński's moaning. He was very bright. His formal schooling as a child had been rather limited – he'd had to make do with what was available in the village's elementary school – but that didn't bother him because farming was what he was interested in and what he wanted to do. At twenty-one he went off to do his military service. At twenty-nine he enrolled at an agricultural college, and he not only completed the course satisfactorily but really absorbed what he'd learned. In particular he developed a keen interest in the best ways of propagating desirable strains of vegetables and fruit trees. Happy to volunteer for public service and support anything that would help the community, he took a turn as manager of the village's dairy co-operative. He was also involved in the discussions with Ignacy Solarz which resulted in the formation in 1935 of a health co-operative in Markowa – the first in Poland.

As Józef reached maturity and began to think about getting married he had to face in a painfully personal way one of the worrying consequences of the imbalance between Poland's population and its economy. The share of the family farm which he inherited was only about two acres. To make the best possible living from it he used half the land to set up a fruit-tree nursery. It was the first of its kind in Markowa. He was able to generate a steady income from the sale of saplings and became expert in grafting apple trees. Józef also practised beekeeping and the raising of silkworms, and in 1933 he won a prize in an agricultural exhibition for inventing and making new types of hives and tools for apiculture. Prince Andrzej Lubomirski, a major landowner and

Józef Ulma

hereditary proprietor of Przeworsk, made a visit to the Ulma farm to see for himself Józef's silkworms and the mulberry trees he was growing for them to feed on. This prince was a well-known enthusiast for every kind of agricultural improvement and rural industrial enterprise, and his family estate was considered the best-developed in Galicia. In common with many other Polish villages Markowa didn't yet have electricity, but Józef built a small wind-powered generator and connected it to a light bulb. This made the Ulma house the first in Markowa to enjoy the benefit of electric light.

Józef loved reading and had a small collection of books which he happily lent out to anyone who was interested, acting as a kind of librarian to the various groups he belonged to. Another of his big interests in life was photography. Hardly anyone in rural Poland at that time had a camera, but Józef made one for himself and later acquired a really good professional one. He also fitted up a makeshift darkroom to do his own developing. Photography became another source of income, because everyone wanted to have their picture taken or to commission Józef to take photos at their families' weddings, first communions and christenings. The local Wici had an amateur dramatics group, so he sometimes took part in theatrical productions, and it was during rehearsals that he got to know Wiktoria Niemczak. One year when they were putting on a nativity play Wiktoria got the part of Mary. Though twelve years younger than Józef she shared his interest in learning new things, having taken several courses at the Orkan University, and they got on well. Their friendship soon turned to love, and they were married at St Dorota's in July 1935. Their first child arrived a year later: a little girl whom they named Stanisława – or Stasia for short. Another daughter, Barbara (Basia), was born in October 1937, and they welcomed a son, Władysław (Władziu), in June 1938.

Wiktoria and Józef Ulma

The Summer of 1939

Notwithstanding Józef's entrepreneurial management of his smallholding, supporting a growing family on a two-acre farm was far from ideal. No additional land was to be had in Markowa, but they worked out that if he and Wiktoria sold the land they had, and put the proceeds together with some savings they'd put aside, they'd be able to afford a larger property at the far eastern end of the province. It would be a wrench to leave Markowa, but they were sure they'd be doing the right thing to up stakes and move. Accordingly, they'd begun the process of purchasing a twelve-acre farm in a village near Sokal. Besides covering a much larger area, the fields there were rich in "black earth", which is unusually fertile. The Ulmas were looking forward excitedly to the forthcoming big change in their lives.

Josek Riesenbach, then nine years old, belonged to one of Markowa's most prosperous Jewish families. They had a small farm but were also engaged in trading: Josek's father Jakub dealt in livestock during the winter and fruit during the summer, and his mother Ita ran a small general store which sold fresh and tinned food, and other useful items including fabric for making clothes. They had a largeish house with a warehouse adjoining, and because there was no synagogue in Markowa theirs was one of three places in the village which was used as a house of prayer. One room was set aside to be used for services, and a Torah scroll was kept there. For the High Holidays, the Markowa Jews attended the synagogue in Łańcut, which was still the nearest town and about five miles away. Almost a third of Łańcut's population was Jewish. As the eldest Riesenbach child, Josek was responsible for looking after the house when the adults were busy working; this involved keeping things clean and preparing meals for himself and his two little sisters, Mania and Genia, and also feeding and mucking out the farm animals.

Both these families – the Ulmas and the Riesenbachs – in their different ways were happy and content. They felt confident about who they were and what they wanted in life, and had no fears for the future. They had no idea how dramatically their world was about to be turned upside down.

Blitzkrieg

Early in the morning of 1st September 1939, units of the German army which had been poised ready at several points along the frontier raced across and into western Poland, while the Luftwaffe rained down bombs on Polish cities and columns of refugees seeking to escape from the destruction. There had been no warning and no declaration of war. The Polish army didn't stand a chance, but nevertheless put up a courageous defence, seeking to delay the German advance for a few days at least until Britain and France could come to the rescue. Poland was one of the least motorised countries in Europe and its army remained heavily dependent on cavalry. This led to the creation of a myth of romantic but totally out-of-date Polish cavalrymen charging panzer tanks, but this was a complete misunderstanding of what was going on. Horses were used primarily for mobility, to get the cavalrymen into good positions from which to fight as infantry. Properly deployed, Polish cavalry units could, and did, play a crucial role in holding up the advance of the German tanks.

Britain and France immediately issued ultimatums, which Hitler ignored, and when these expired on 3rd September declared war on Germany, but no immediate assistance was forthcoming. On 17th September the Soviet Union, as part of a secret deal agreed between Ribbentrop, acting for Hitler, and Molotov acting for Stalin, invaded Poland from the east. Under cover of the military activity, while the two ruthless dictatorships were slicing up the country between them, they took steps to deal with any potential opposition. Thousands of Polish officers and other prisoners of war were massacred by the Soviets, and an estimated half a million civilians – including whole families with small children – arrested and packed off to prison camps in Siberia. In the area overrun by Germany, Einsatzgruppen (special task groups) moved in with lists of Polish intellectuals and leading cultural figures – politicians and academics, actors and writers, doctors and priests, businessmen and landowners – rounding up about 20,000 people and shooting them.

Nazi ideology deemed Poles, along with all Slavs, to be racially inferior – effectively sub-human and fit only to be slaves. October 1939 saw the German-ruled area divided into two sections. The regions adjoining Germany were annexed to the Reich and became officially part of Germany. Although their population was nearly ninety

German soldiers invade Poland on 1st September 1939

per cent Polish, the plan was to Germanise them through bringing in ethnic German settlers, encouraging Poles of German ancestry to apply for "Volksdeutsch" status as ethnic Germans, and gradually expelling everyone else into the non-annexed region. Polish Catholicism in the annexed regions was targeted for annihilation as a matter of top priority. Most of the bishops and clergy were arrested and then deported into the non-annexed region, sent to concentration camps or simply shot. Convents were closed, and hundreds of nuns were sent to concentration camps or transferred to Germany for forced labour.

The General Government

The non-annexed part, which included Galicia, became what was called the General Government. It was to be administered as a kind of colony and slave labour pool. Most governmental structures which had not collapsed were summarily abolished except at the very lowest levels. In Polish villages, the sołtys (the village head) was left in place, but whereas previously the sołtys had been the elected leader of the village's self-governing council, he instead became a tool of the occupation and was required to implement German directives without question. If he objected or sought to resign, he'd be threatened with imprisonment.

Contingents of German police were brought in to carry out routine policing and maintenance of public order, but it quickly became apparent that they didn't have sufficient manpower, so all former Polish policemen were ordered to report for duty. Under threat of severe punishment, they mostly did so, but almost immediately a process began of remodelling the Polish police force to bring it fully under Nazi control. Their commanding officers were dismissed or demoted, and anyone showing too much decency, and reluctance to participate in the brutal enforcement of Nazi policies – especially the "Jewish regulations" – was removed and replaced by others who were less scrupulous. Because they wore dark-blue uniforms they were known as the Blue Police. They worked under the supervision of the German police, who wore green uniforms and were known as the Green Police.

Poles were liable to be seized at any time and sent to Germany for forced labour, unpaid and under appalling conditions. Many others were arrested and sent to concentration camps. Farming families were by and large left to continue growing food, out of which a hefty quota could be requisitioned to feed the German "master race". Among the effects of the German occupation was a general enabling and fostering of criminality and violence: the official food ration for Poles was insufficient to sustain life, so everyone had to depend on the black market to survive, and hooligans of all kinds quickly learned that they could harass Jews with impunity. Another was pervasive terror: any action seen as against German interests could result in savage reprisals with dozens of Poles being seized at random and taken away to be shot. Paradoxically, the Catholic Church in the General Government was allowed to function more or less normally – perhaps Hitler saw it as a cheap way of keeping the slaves happy.

The Polish Jews numbered 3.3 million – roughly ten per cent of the total population of interwar Poland. What the Nazis had in mind for them was even worse than for the Poles, though at this early stage the distinction was barely apparent. Synagogues were blown up or burned down, and rabbis were singled out for public humiliation and ridicule. All Jews living in the regions annexed to Germany were expelled into the General Government, where, in the main cities and towns, measures were quickly initiated to separate them off from everyone else by herding them into closed-off ghettoes. They were forbidden to use public transport, a decree was issued that they must all wear a white armband with a blue Star of David, and the men and older boys were subject to forced labour. As more and more people were crammed into the ghettoes they became dangerously overcrowded, and food supplies were deliberately kept short, with the aim of ensuring that as many Jews as possible died of "natural causes" through malnutrition and disease.

The Sanacja regime was completely discredited, and its leaders had fled. A Polish government-in-exile was established in London under Władysław Sikorski, who'd been one of the opposition leaders. Within Poland a resistance movement was organised which maintained communications with the government-in-exile and was answerable to it. Its armed wing – the Home Army – carried out acts of sabotage, though with extreme caution because of the savage reprisals wreaked on the civilian population. The Home Army also operated its own secret courts and justice system. and had ways of imposing sanctions on Poles guilty of collaboration with the Germans, up to and including the death penalty for particularly egregious crimes against the community. A wide range of – often spontaneous – forms of resistance and non-collaboration helped keep up Polish morale. Polish railway workers would quietly disable locomotives to bring the Germans' military transportation to a standstill, and factory workers managed to turn out remarkably high proportions of defective articles. Young people studied in underground secondary schools and universities. As we know, Karol Wojtyła pursued his training for the priesthood in an underground seminary. Educating Poles was, however, treated as a very serious crime, and teachers who were caught were sent to Auschwitz.

The invasions as seen from Łańcut and Markowa

Rzeszów, a larger and more important town than Łańcut lying about ten miles or so to the west, was taken by the German army on 8th September 1939. The Polish government functionaries in Łańcut immediately abandoned their posts in terror. Count Alfred Potocki, the hereditary proprietor, stepped in and formed an ad hoc town council to hold things together and avert chaos, and to organise assistance for the refugees flooding in from Rzeszów and the growing numbers of wounded Polish soldiers. The first German patrols entered Łańcut at dawn on 10th September. The commanding officers and their staff were swiftly billeted in the castle, taking over most of it, although Count Alfred was allowed to continue living in a few rooms on the ground floor. An order went out that the Jewish shops must be marked with a Star of David, making them targets for depredation. The beautiful eighteenth-century synagogue was set on fire, but Count Alfred sent the fire brigade to put out the flames, and the building was saved.

Meanwhile the German forces were pressing on towards the San River about twenty miles to the east, where Polish forces were preparing to make a stand at Przemyśl. The river, which runs through the centre of the city, was the demarcation line agreed between Ribbentrop and Molotov, but the Poles were still unaware of the secret pact. They managed to hold the invaders off for four days, but during the evening of 14th September orders arrived to abandon the city and withdraw eastwards, blowing up the bridges behind them. German soldiers entered Przemyśl the next morning, accompanied by an Einsatzgruppe which commenced to massacre the Jews. Over five hundred were slaughtered, and the rest were forced across the San to the side of the city which was to become part of the Soviet Zone. Before withdrawing to their side, the Germans burned down the Old Synagogue, which dated back to 1594, and the Tempel Synagogue.

On 22nd September, an order was issued expelling the Jews of Łańcut from the town, telling them to head east. This only happened in towns that were relatively close to the San: it didn't apply to the large Jewish community of Rzeszów, where they comprised about half the town's population. It was supposed to apply to the Jews living in Markowa and nearby villages, but the situation was fairly chaotic, and although a few families left their homes and sought to comply, most stayed put. Even in Łańcut, Count Alfred managed to obtain exemptions from expulsion for a small number who, he argued, were essential workers. The idea was to send the Jews into what would become the Soviet Zone, and some of them did end up there, but most were turned back by Soviet patrols as they approached the border. They somehow managed to find shelter in villages and hamlets along the way and in November began trickling back into the town. Their homes had been looted and their businesses closed or expropriated, but rather than being re-expelled they were registered for forced labour. To make it easier to keep an eye on them they were all moved into one part of the town. The number of Jews in Łańcut and Rzeszów actually went up, because these were among the places to which Jews expelled from the German-annexed regions were sent.

Josek Riesenbach's experience of the start of the occupation began with seeing planes flying overhead and hearing the sound of shooting. Soon after that, some villagers – not close neighbours but definitely locals – burned down the Riesenbach warehouse. Josek was no longer allowed to go to school, but he didn't mind too much because the Polish boys had always bullied him for being Jewish. Some of the measures decreed for Jews generally – like wearing Star of David armbands and being registered for forced labour – applied in Markowa, but the village Jews were mostly able to remain in their own homes and continue to make a living. Their family belongings did, however, become liable to summary confiscation: any valuables were quickly seized, as were blankets and anything made with fur. During the winter months, as Josek would later recall, he and his father, along with other villagers, were made to go with spades to clear snow off the main roads. This often entailed having to travel for several miles to reach the designated worksite, and doing so on foot: there was never any question of the Germans providing transport.

A Blue Police station was established in Markowa under the command of Konstanty Kindler, a Volksdeutsch from the part of Poland annexed to Germany, who had become a keen Nazi and soon made himself notorious for his brutality and rapacity. He made the most of the opportunity to practise extortion on the village Jews, particularly targeting the Goldmans. The Blue Police station was quite near the Ulmas' house – just a few hundred yards away. Before the end of 1939, Markowa was expected to find accommodation for 514 Poles expelled from the German-annexed regions. The young men of the village became liable to seizure for forced labour, and 118 of them were taken and sent to Germany. Some community leaders who had been serving as officers in the Polish army were missing and would never return. Captain Władisław Ciekot fell victim to the mass murders carried out in the spring of 1940 by the NKVD – the Soviet secret police – in the Forest of Katyń, and Major Antoni Flejszar, who'd four times been awarded the Cross of Valour, was killed around the same time in a linked massacre inside a prison in Kharkiv. Ignacy Solarz was arrested by the Gestapo in February 1940 and is assumed to have been killed soon afterwards, though his body was never found.

Life under Occupation

Józef Ulma had been called up when the war broke out but had come home safely. He and his family were poorer now than before because their new farm was in the Soviet Zone, so the savings they'd sunk into it were lost. Thankfully, however, they still had their old home and smallholding, and they knew there were many people far worse off. Among other ways of earning money, Józef continued with his little photography business. The German government was gradually issuing people with new identity documents known as kennkarten, and a kennkarte needed a photograph. Kennkarten were actually quite easy to forge, so Józef's skills were in demand both for genuine kennkarten and for false ones, which could come in handy for all kinds of purposes including resistance activities.

In Łańcut, Count Alfred and his mother Elizabeth used their resources to support a soup kitchen at the Convent of the Sisters of Mercy of St Charles Borromeo, which provided four hundred meals a day to people arriving destitute after being expelled from the German-annexed regions. They also created a substantial number of jobs (many fictitious) on their estate and around the castle and grounds, partly to give people the chance to earn some income but also to protect them from seizure for forced labour. Luckily the most senior of the German officers billeted in the castle seem not to have been much enamoured of the Nazis; certainly they treated the family with respect and were inclined to turn a blind eye to some of what they were up to. (It can't have hurt that Elizabeth was by origin a princess of the Radziwiłł family and related to the Hohenzollerns, the dynasty that had ruled Prussia and the German Empire up to 1918.) The Germans even responded positively to the Count's interventions on behalf of people who'd been arrested, although he had to be very discreet about that, and the details are rarely clear. It's possible that he paid a ransom to ease their release. A large quota of the food produced by his estate was, of course, earmarked for German use, but this gave him leverage: he could argue that an arrestee was one of his essential workers, without whom the quota couldn't be met.

In the early stages of the occupation the Potockis' relief efforts had been extended to all Poles, Catholics and Jews alike. When the Jews were registered and separated off, Count Alfred initially tried to extend assistance openly to them, but the Germans quickly forbade that. The Jewish families in Łańcut could have taken advantage of the soup kitchen at the convent but rarely did, probably because it was too risky for them to venture outside their homes. They did run their own soup kitchen and bakery in a small Hassidic house of prayer, and from time to time Count Alfred quietly sent deliveries of potatoes to help with that.

Policing and surveillance

The Nazis were naturally interested to learn of Markowa's German antecedents, and over the next year or so devoted considerable time and energy to conducting pseudo-scientific studies involving the shape and measurements of the villagers' heads. As a result, Markowa was identified as suitable for Germanification, something which could have ensured more favourable treatment for some, though not all, of the inhabitants. However, only two residents proved willing to sign up for Volksdeutsch status. Kindler meanwhile progressed from robbery-with-menaces to killing. He would eagerly volunteer to perform executions, and he is known to have murdered an elderly Jew in the village. From January 1941 a Green Police station was established in Łańcut, headed by Leutnant Eilert Dieken. Among the officers assigned to serve under his command was Josef Kokott, a Germanised Czech: Kokott would remain in Łańcut throughout the remainder of the occupation. The Green Police presence ensured closer supervision of the activities of the Blue Police and further limited any room they had for soft-pedalling the more horrific German directives. This must have pleased Kindler no end and inspired him to even greater zeal in pursuance of his big ambition, which was to achieve promotion to the Green Police.

It wasn't possible for the German occupation authorities to maintain continuous, hands-on control over villages like Markowa in the way they could in the big cities. The main form of local transportation in rural areas of Poland continued to be horse-drawn. Even the German army had limited numbers of motor vehicles and was partly dependent on horses, and because motors had been relatively scarce even before the war in what became the General Government, there hadn't been many available to confiscate. Whenever transport was needed, orders would be sent to the villages requiring them to provide so many carts with drivers. To succeed in enforcing their regulations in the countryside the Germans therefore had to rely on Polish collaborators – voluntary or coerced.

Everyday surveillance was delegated to the Blue Police assisted by the sołtys and a network of auxiliaries who, for the most part, were probably coerced: specially appointed "village guards" and the voluntary firefighters. Additionally, the Germans nominated hostages – village residents who were liable to be shot if the community was found to be involved in any anti-German activities

– and the hostages were treated as additional manpower to be deployed in carrying out surveillance. In Markowa the village guards were commanded by Andrzej Rewer, who was also a named hostage, and the firefighters by Franciszek Homa. The fact that the Green Police in Łańcut used horse-drawn vehicles to move around meant that, although they made periodic inspection visits to Markowa, the chances of them suddenly appearing in the village without any warning were slight. On the other hand, there were certain residents who seemed to be on surprisingly good terms with the Germans, and who were generally believed to be acting as informers.

What would I do?

No large group of people is monolithic, with everyone thinking and reacting the same way. Under the German occupation of 1939-45, with all the problems and threats they themselves were facing, individual Poles reacted very differently to what they saw happening to the Jews. There were those who welcomed the opportunity to collaborate with the Nazis to get rid of their Jewish neighbours and seize their houses, business assets and other possessions. The Blue Police and their auxiliaries were expected to enforce the Jewish regulations and show suitable enthusiasm in doing so. Some of them undoubtedly tried to find ways of appearing zealously busy without actually getting anything done, but that was a difficult line to tread and meant living in fear that one of their colleagues might notice and report them.

No doubt most people kept their heads down and concentrated on their own daily struggles to make ends meet, but the plight of the Jews might still throw up tempting opportunities. There were rewards to be gained by denouncing Jews who had gone into hiding, or else there was the option of blackmailing them, demanding payment in return for not betraying them. Blackmailings and denunciations of Jews could, of course, incur punishment at the hands of the Resistance, and there were well-publicised cases of blackmailers being executed by the Home Army. However, such cases were difficult to investigate and hardly the Resistance's top priority, so there was a good chance of getting away with it.

Research suggests that the overwhelming majority of Polish people resisted temptations to harm the Jews or exploit their vulnerability, and at least kept their hands clean, but didn't feel obliged to make any positive efforts to help them. They'd have felt that they had enough problems of their own and that the Jews were really nothing to do with them anyway. Moreover, Poles who did try to offer help to the Jews, or show signs of sympathy with their plight, soon discovered that it could get them into quite serious trouble. They might also incur disapproval from their neighbours, especially if the neighbours feared being drawn into the trouble.

It's never too difficult to provide a bit of help to other people (and make myself feel good) by giving away some spare cash. But what if I didn't have enough for myself? Would it be fair to give anything away if my family didn't have enough? What if my act of kindness led to my being fined or sent to prison? What if it led to everyone else in my street giving me dirty looks and muttering about me behind my back, not wanting to be associated with me in case I brought reprisals down on their heads too?

If I were in that situation, what would I do?

Operation Barbarossa

On 22nd June 1941, once again in the early hours of the morning and without any warning or declaration of war, German planes began bombing cities in the Soviet-occupied part of Poland, and three million Wehrmacht troops crossed the border into Soviet territory. Hitler had decreed a war of annihilation against Communism, and Einsatzgruppen followed closely behind. Their orders were that any political commissars or partisans who were captured were to be shot immediately without trial, and all Jews – regardless of sex or age – were to be regarded as partisans. The numbers designated for slaughter were massive. Partly due to their heavy workload and partly as a deliberate policy, the Einsatzgruppen set about involving ordinary German soldiers and policemen in the killings. It proved frighteningly easy to convince them that they had a moral duty to perform their fair share of what was presented to them as an admittedly distasteful task but one which, nevertheless, was a "military necessity".

Local people were also induced to participate. In the early stages, the invasion forces were passing through non-Russian territories whose people had never wanted to be part of the Soviet Union and who'd come to loathe bitterly their Soviet masters. These people usually had a history of generalised anti-Semitism, but they'd also developed a deep-seated conviction that all Jews were pro-Communist, so a legitimate target for revenge. It was in this context that in Jedwabne a mob of about 40 ethnic Poles murdered at least 340 of their Jewish fellow-townspeople. Most of the victims – men, women and children – were locked in a barn which was then set on fire. In Lwów and other cities, Ukrainian nationalists, who'd been led to believe that the Nazis were supportive of their aspirations for Ukrainian independence, carried out fearsome pogroms in which thousands of Jews died and many others were left badly injured.

Throughout the second half of 1941 and into the following year the sołtyś of Markowa, Andrzej Kud, dealt with frequent requisition orders for horse-drawn wagons to transport military equipment to the Eastern Front. German contingents occasionally passed through Markowa on their way there, and some of them were billeted in the Riesenbachs' house. The first group that came were regular army officers, and they were friendly and quite well-behaved. After them came a Gestapo unit which stayed for about four weeks, during which time the family were thrown out of their home. The next group to arrive were SS: they made Ita cook and clean for them, and the little girls, Mania and Genia, were made to help with that, while Jakub and Josek cleaned their equipment and boots. However, they inflicted nothing worse on the family, and once they'd moved on the Riesenbachs got their home back.

Far more terrible things were already happening elsewhere, and Ita and Jakub are likely to have heard something about those things even if the children hadn't. In Łańcut, former Jewish residents who'd been expelled into the Soviet-occupied territory saw the invasion as an opportunity to slip back home, only to discover that they were all now suspected of being pro-Communist. A number of them were arrested and shot. Encouraged by the ease with which they were getting away with murder in Soviet territory, the Nazis felt that the time had come to raise the stakes in the General Government. All the larger concentrations of Jews had by this time been rounded up and ghettoised, in sections of cities and towns sealed off by walls or barbed wire, with the entrances closely guarded and any windows overlooking the outside world boarded up. Many towns had not yet been dealt with, but in June a ghetto area was marked out in Rzeszów, and the Jews there began to be moved into it. On 15th October 1941, a decree was issued that any Jews caught trying to escape the ghettoes or hide would incur the death penalty – and that the same would apply to any Pole who helped by providing shelter or supplying food. The Blue Police were expected to enforce these regulations and were often tasked with carrying out the executions. At first some of them were reluctant, but they soon got used to it.

The final solution

Early in 1942, secret plans were laid down for the total extermination of the Jews. Death camps were set up in the General Government at Bełżec, Sobibór and Treblinka, with facilities for mass murder, and similar facilities were added at the concentration camp of Majdanek and at Auschwitz II-Birkenau in German-annexed Silesia. All the ghettoes had good railway connections – their locations had been selected with that in mind – and from March onwards the people imprisoned in them began to be summoned to assemble with their luggage to board trains. They were told that they were being evacuated for "resettlement in the east". Many of them at first believed that, or hoped it was true: nobody knew for sure. The trains were made up of cattle trucks into each of which a hundred people would be squeezed. Locked in, they were often left without food or water during a journey that could last days. The larger ghettoes in the big cities were the first to be evacuated. Rzeszów was quite a long way down the priority list. Meanwhile contingents of Jews from Łańcut and other unghettoised towns round about began to be brought in carts and forced into the

Rzeszów ghetto, making it so overcrowded that, by early July, families were crammed three to a room.

During that month, the Rzeszów ghetto was emptied out. Most of the inhabitants were sent to Bełżec to be put to death in the gas chambers, but about a thousand who were old and frail, sick, or disabled were taken into the Rodna forest and murdered there. Once Jews were trapped in sealed ghettoes it was very difficult to escape or hide: any who attempted to do so were almost always caught and shot. In Łańcut, however, when the date for evacuation was announced, quite a number managed to find hiding places. On 3rd August those who hadn't were loaded into carts and sent away under armed guard to a transit camp in Pelkinie village, about twenty miles away towards the north-east, where a sorting-out process took place. The young and strong were sent to forced labour camps, and a few were even allowed to return temporarily to Łańcut to be available for forced labour there. Of the rest, some were transported to Bełżec, but the old and sick were shot in or near the camp, and the children led off to the Nechczioli forest a few miles away, where they were clubbed to death to save bullets.

Some of the Jews in Łańcut who managed to hide received help from Polish Catholics to do so. One member of the Blue Police took Kalman Wolkenfeld and his wife and child to the flat he shared with a couple in their fifties, Michał and Aniela Nizioł, and asked if they could stay there. Everyone knew the Wolkenfelds, who ran a popular restaurant in the town. Michał responded that they would certainly not leave a family with a child to die, and they were taken in and carefully hidden. However, someone denounced the Niziołs. Michał was out when the police arrived. Thanks to the tip-off, the police found the Jews right away, took them out and shot them. Aniela was taken to the police station and interrogated, but then released. She chose to return home, despite anxious neighbours pleading with her to go into hiding herself – as Michał had done as soon as he heard what had happened – though she also seized the opportunity to go to confession and receive Holy Communion. The next day, 24th August, the Green Police arrived. Josef Kokott took Aniela out into the courtyard and shot her.

The execution of Aniela Nizioł had been carried out in the open so that people would see and take warning: this was what happened to anyone who tried to help the Jews. Despite this terrifying "example", at least one household in Łańcut is known to have continued to hide Jews. The Gwizdak family who ran a bakery in the town had agreed in July to provide shelter to two fugitives, one of whom was an old friend from before the war, and over the next couple of years they took in four more. Through them, six lives were saved. Understandably, however, other people who were hiding Jews weren't prepared to take the risk, and forced their guests to leave. Włodzimierz Leś, a constable in the Blue Police who lived on the outskirts of Łańcut, had agreed a deal with the Szall family to help them go into hiding, in return for the Szalls making over their assets to him. The name of the father of this family was Szall (Saul) Goldman, but he'd come to use Szall as his family name. Then in his late sixties, he'd previously been a prosperous cattle dealer. With him in hiding were his four adult sons, Baruch, Mechel, Joachim and Mojsze (Moses), but their mother Golda had somehow become separated from them and had been captured, then shot near the market place by Kokott. When Leś realised that the Germans really were going to apply the death penalty to anyone found helping Jews, he went back on his promise and told the Szalls to find somewhere else to stay – but he didn't return their property.

Hiding in the fields and in the ravines

The Jews in Markowa had been told to apply for kennkarten and given a deadline for doing so: 30th April 1942. Whereas Poles received grey kennkarten, Jews were given yellow ones. The application process allowed the Germans to compile a register of all the Jews in the village, in preparation for their removal. The sequence of events from then until the end of 1942 is difficult to pin down – everyone was frightened and confused, different people recalled things differently, and for many of the incidents there are no surviving eyewitnesses – so any account is necessarily tentative. The first killings seem to have taken place in late July. Some Germans came to the village and made straight for Kazimierz, the part of Markowa that had been most heavily Jewish before the war, but they could only find about a dozen people. Those captured were lined up on a plot of land belonging to a Jewish farmer, Beniem Müller, and shot.

In early August, two members of the Blue Police who'd been friendly with Jakub Riesenbach came to warn him to flee, because they'd received orders from the Germans to round up all the Jews. The family left immediately, taking nothing with them except the Torah scroll, and hid in the fields. Other Jews in the village may also have received warnings, as most of them managed to hide. The Germans arrived the next day, having requisitioned a number of carts with drivers, and announced that Jews were no longer permitted to remain in this part of Poland, and that those in Markowa were to be sent for "resettlement". However only about six or eight could be found to board the carts, mostly elderly people who felt that they had no choice. Even after the Germans had left, the rest of the Jews didn't dare return to their homes. Some managed to find refuge with peasant families, some stayed in stables or barns without seeking the permission of the owners, while others continued to hide in the fields, on the edges of the forested areas, or in the ravines down by the stream.

The number of children in the Ulma household had grown to five, with the addition of Franciszek (Franuś), born in April 1940, and Antoni (Antoś), born in June 1941. Józef Ulma helped Rifka Tencer, who was hiding in a ravine with her two daughters and a small granddaughter, to build a dugout to provide better shelter. After Leś turned out the Szalls to fend for themselves, they made their way to Markowa and sought help from Józef, who was someone they knew, and he agreed to take them in and hide them. Wiktoria was pregnant again: a sixth child, Marysia, was born in September 1942.

The Ulma children

Around that time, the family also took in the Goldmans'
two older married daughters: Layka Didner, who had
a little girl with her, and Golda Grünfeld. Chaim and
Estera Goldman, probably together with their younger
children, had taken refuge in a neighbouring village
named Zabratówka, where at some point they must have
been discovered and killed, because they did not survive
the war.

The Riesenbachs are given refuge

For two months the Riesenbachs lived rough in the
open. During the day they'd lie down, making sure
they couldn't be seen behind the standing corn or the
dense foliage of the potato plants. At night, Jakub and
Ita went around calling on the families they'd been
best acquainted with, trying to find someone who was
willing to take them in. The Kielar family, who'd been
their neighbours when they were in their home, agreed
to look after Mania and Genia at least for a short while:
the little girls were hidden in their attic. Eventually the
Riesenbach parents tried the house of Józef and Julia
Bar. The Bars were terrified: they knew that if they
agreed to shelter Jews, they could be shot along with
their 19-year-old daughter Janina. Nevertheless, they
gave in to the pleading and agreed to take the family
in – though only, Józef insisted, for a few months until
they could find somewhere else. Shortly after this, Ita

had a dream which led her to believe that the girls were in danger, so she went to fetch them and move them to the Bar house. As it turned out, she was just in time: the Germans had been tipped off, and a few hours later the Kielars' house was raided.

The Riesenbachs promised to give everything they owned to the Bars after the war. However, it wasn't really a question of money, especially given the uncertainty as to whether any of them would still be alive. It certainly wasn't a question of blackmail, but more like a debt of honour: the Bars were desperately poor and could hardly feed themselves, let alone feed five more. Nevertheless, they shared everything they had with the guests who were hidden in their attic. Julia – described by Josek many years later as a tiny woman who was a devout Christian – used to say that whatever happens is the will of God. Janina had fully accepted the situation, and it was mainly she who brought the Riesenbachs their meals. Although initially Józef Bar had been reluctant to take the Riesenbachs in at all, before long he'd grown as concerned for their safety as for that of his own family, and as an added precaution he'd built a bunker in the cellar. At any sign of danger, they were to run and hide in there, and he'd pile potatoes up over the entrance. Neither the attic nor the cellar was heated, and it was bitterly cold down in the cellar, but being cold was better than being dead. During the day when the Bars were out working in their fields, and provided there was nobody else around, the Riesenbachs were allowed to come down into the main part of the house to stretch their legs and be more comfortable.

Due to having compiled a register, the Germans knew that most of the Markowa Jews were still unaccounted for. The Blue Police, village guards, firefighters and hostages were under strict orders to track down the hidden Jews and hand them in. From time to time someone was found, captured, dragged to the nearest road, and shot. To what extent the hunters did their work willingly is impossible to determine; reprisals by the Germans, if they realised their orders were being disobeyed, could be savage. As winter approached, it became more and more difficult to survive in the open. One woman is known to have died of exposure, and at least one man gave himself up to the hunters, deciding to take his chances with the Germans rather than freeze to death. A number of households in Markowa were by that point looking after hidden Jews, but they had to be very careful: they knew that there were fellow villagers, not to mention outsiders like Kindler, who would betray them if they heard of anything.

Karski's mission

In the summer of 1942, Jan Karski, an experienced courier for the Polish Resistance, was given a special and very important mission – his last mission as it happened, because he would never be able to return to Poland afterwards. He was selected for his well-attested tradecraft skills and courage, and because he was known to have a photographic memory. He would be carrying microfilm evidence of what was being done to the Jews, but he was also to be prepared to give eye-witness testimony. Accordingly, in August, he was smuggled into the Warsaw Ghetto to witness the terrible conditions there – starving children, bodies lying in the streets, people staring vacantly because they had no more hope. Next, Karski was smuggled into what he thought was the main death camp at Bełżec, but which was in fact one of its satellites, the Izbica transit camp. There he saw Jews being forced onto trains to take them to the gas chambers. As he readied himself to depart on his mission he arranged to have some of his teeth extracted so that his swollen gums would provide an excuse not to reply if he were stopped at a checkpoint. Finally, a priest brought a pyx containing the Blessed Sacrament and hung it round his neck, so that Our Lord would travel with him and bring him safely to his destination.

In disguise and making use of false papers, Karski had somehow to cross through Germany, then through Vichy France and into neutral Spain, eventually reaching Gibraltar from where he could secure passage by sea to England. Successfully making it to London, he delivered his microfilm as instructed. On 10th December 1942, the Polish government-in-exile published a report – "The Mass Extermination of Jews in German-Occupied Poland". A week later the governments of the Allied nations issued a declaration condemning "in the strongest possible terms this bestial policy of cold-blooded extermination" and pledging retribution for those responsible. In the House of Commons, the foreign secretary, Anthony Eden, read out the declaration, and the MPs stood in silence to express their solidarity. The declaration was broadcast to the nation that evening by the BBC. The Feast of the Immaculate Conception was observed in the UK as a day of prayer for Poland, and Cardinal Hinsley, preaching at a Mass in Westminster Cathedral celebrated by an exiled Polish bishop, spoke out against "the brutal persecution of the Jews" and appealed to the "civilised world" to put an end to the "wholesale campaign of extermination" being perpetrated on Polish soil.

Efforts to help

Meetings were set up for Karski to testify directly to leading politicians and journalists in the UK and the USA, including Anthony Eden and President Roosevelt. He pleaded for the Allies to take action to save the Jews and was heartbroken when nothing was done. Szmul Ziegielbojm, one of two Jewish members of the Polish government-in-exile, committed suicide as a protest against what he saw as the Allied leaders' indifference to the fate of the Jews. Roosevelt and Churchill were, however, convinced that at that stage in the war there was absolutely nothing they could do to stop the Holocaust, and they were probably right. The only people who could help were people actually on the ground, and those in Poland could only do so in strictest secrecy and very much at the risk of their own lives.

An underground network – Żegota – was set up as part of the Polish Resistance to provide assistance to the Jews. Żegota provided food, medicines, money and false documents to thousands of Jews – mainly those who'd managed to hide, but also some of those held in forced labour camps. Jews in hiding, unless they could pass as Aryans, were unable to work and weren't entitled to rations, so help with food was vital. Żegota also placed around 2,500 Jewish children with foster families or in church-run orphanages, where they had to learn Christian prayers so that they could pretend to be Polish Catholics. Despite huge difficulties in doing so, the Polish government-in-exile was constantly trying to send funds to support underground activities. From May 1943 it began allocating some of the funds to Żegota and other organisations seeking to rescue Jews, and this allocation was steadily increased as the war dragged on. As well as the organised groups, there were the Polish individuals and families who hid and looked after Jews, including, no doubt, many whose names are now known only to God. Set against the scale of the Holocaust, the number of lives they could save seems tiny, but we must never lose sight of the deep truth in the precept given to us through Jewish teaching that "whoever saves a single life saves an entire universe".

The Bone Yard

As 1942 drew to a close, the German authorities charged with mopping up any Jews remaining in the Polish countryside were losing patience. In Markowa, the sołtyś, Andrzej Kud, received orders to conduct a thorough search of all possible hiding places in and around the village on Sunday 13th December. It was Kud's practice to stand outside the church after the main morning Mass each Sunday to make announcements, and on that Sunday he spoke about the impending search, stressing the vital importance of ensuring that all the Jews be found and turned in. After the war, he would argue that he'd done that in order to ensure that everyone was properly warned and could better camouflage the hiding places. The Bar family got themselves home from Mass as quickly as they could and took the Riesenbachs down into the cellar.

The search began in the afternoon with at least twenty-six participants – Blue Police, forest guards, firefighters, hostages and possibly a few co-opted others.

This was enough to search the village but not enough to make more than a perfunctory search of the surrounding fields and countryside. They used dogs: the Riesenbachs, cowering and shivering in the cellar, could hear them barking. Józef Bar opened his front door to find four men who asked whether he was hiding any Jews. He invited them to come and see for themselves, opened the trap door to the cellar and went down, gesturing to them to follow. Down in the cellar there were potatoes piled on one side and animal feed on the other, and at the end facing the stairs a shelf with bottles of home-brewed spirit. Józef told the men he was trying out a new recipe and offered them samples, which served to distract them from their purpose. After a couple of minutes' friendly chat, the searchers left.

Though the Riesenbachs and others remained safely hidden and were not found, not everyone was so lucky. About twenty-five Jews are thought to have been captured, including Rifka Tencer and her family. A girl named Idka was found but managed to escape and went to Kud's house in hopes of getting help there. This could have led to disaster, as Kud was being obliged to entertain "guests" whom he didn't know and couldn't trust, but he carefully said nothing that could have given Idka away, and she managed to find a hiding place elsewhere. The prisoners were handed over to the Blue Police who brought them to the village crossroads. A basement there in a building belonging to Franciszek Niemczak, Wiktoria Ulma's brother, had for years been rented by the community for use as a temporary lockup when necessary, and the prisoners were pushed in there and left overnight, with Andrzej Rewer standing guard outside. After the war, when he was questioned about this, he said he'd been told that if he didn't obey orders he'd be shot. During the night, the prisoners were heard shouting and praying, and some of them scratched last messages on the walls. In the morning, the Green Police arrived and led them out to a place known as the Bone Yard, which had been used as a burial ground for animals. This site could be seen from the window of the Ulmas' home. A pit had been dug, and the Jews were shot, tipped in and buried. This mass execution seems to have marked the end of the general searches in Markowa: presumably the Germans were satisfied that they'd tracked down all or most of the Jews. Everyone must have breathed a sigh of relief when Kindler took his departure, having won his coveted promotion to the Green Police.

Making ends meet

It's doubtful that the Ulmas' Jewish guests had been able to bring with them any savings, or saleable items, to help pay for their keep. The Szalls did try to retrieve their assets from Leś, but he refused to hand them over. Golda Grünfeld had some gold trinkets in a little box which she kept with her at all times, hidden under her clothing, but they were never sold, so presumably hadn't needed to be. Somehow this crowded little household of sixteen people, half of whom didn't officially exist, was managing to keep itself fed, though Józef's ingenuity must have been stretched to find ways of bringing in enough money. He did develop a profitable sideline in tanning hides, and the Szall brothers were able to help with that. Józef's closest friend Antoni Szpytma is understood to have known that the Ulmas were hiding Jews and provided what help he could.

Józef continued with his photography. People came from quite a wide area around to have their pictures taken – even Włodzimierz Leś turned up one day.

The Ulma children

Besides commissions from paying customers, Józef took numerous pictures of his own beloved wife and children, perhaps to use up the film. Some are posed shots: there's one of Wiktoria and all six children grouped together in a field with sheep grazing nearby and Franuś perched astride one of the sheep. Others show their everyday life: the children playing, or Wiktoria at her household tasks. In one scene she looks as if she might be teaching a small daughter to write. There are also photos of Józef at work. At some point old Szall must have borrowed it to take a photo of his sons, as there's one taken by him of the four of them outside one of the farm buildings, busy sawing up firewood.

Wiktoria teaching her daughter to write

Village of refuge

In January 1943 when the snow lay deep on the ground, Antoni Szylar opened the door of his largeish barn, about twenty yards from his house, to find five Jews hiding there: Miriam Weltz and her four adult children, Mońko, Abraham, Reśka and Aron, together with Aron's wife Shirley. They kissed Antoni's hands and begged him not to drive them away. The Weltzes had been the Szylars' neighbours up to just before the war, when they left Markowa and moved to Jarosław. Antoni was very frightened of the implications for himself, his wife Dorota, and their own five children, Zofia, Helena, Eugeniusz, Franciszek and Janina. Nevertheless, he brought them food and packed plenty of straw around where they were hiding to protect them from the cold. Fairly soon he constructed a kind of plank tunnel in the attic of the house and moved them there. Aron and Shirley's little boy Leon had been taken in by a Polish family in Jarosław, but one day when he was playing in a sandpit their neighbours noticed that he was circumcised, so for safety's sake he was brought to join his parents at the Szylars' home in Markowa. The Szylars were careful not to let anyone know about their guests in the attic not even Antoni's brothers or Helena's fiancé. Eugeniusz, who was twelve, kept a careful watch-out, making sure his playmates never went up in the attic, and whistling a warning if anyone was approaching the house.

In February 1943, Ukrainian nationalists launched a series of massacres against the Polish minority in Volhynia, which subsequently spread into eastern Galicia. Tens of thousands were slaughtered and their villages burned down. Jews and other ethnic minorities, and Ukrainians who tried to rescue them or oppose the violence, were also killed. The occupying Germans had not initiated this campaign, but it suited them actively to encourage it – and in due course to encourage the Poles to take their revenge by killing Ukrainians. Among the victims was Franciszek Homa, formerly head of the Markowa firefighters: he'd moved to a village near Sokal and was murdered there. Terrified refugees flooded westwards, and in the summer of 1943, Markowa gave refuge to 1,600 of them. It was that summer too that Abraham Segal, a thirteen-year-old Jewish boy who'd fled when the Germans murdered the rest of his family, came to Markowa. Passing as a Pole under an assumed name, he found a job working as a shepherd for Jan and Helena Cwynar. The Cwynars realised that he was Jewish, but didn't give him away. They became very fond of him and treated him as one of their own family.

A nosy neighbour of the Szylars visited their house when Antoni wasn't there, climbed the ladder to the attic and saw for himself that there were people hiding up there. This man was known to frequent the local bar, where the men he usually drank with were the ones believed to be informers. When Antoni found out he was very worried and went to consult the local GP, Dr Ignacy Mularek. Dr Mularek already knew about the Weltzes, because he'd been called in when any of them had become ill; he was known to be in the Resistance and trustworthy. Dr Mularek arranged to have a quiet talk with the neighbour to warn him that if he reported anything he'd be in trouble. That seems to have settled the matter: everyone knew what the Home Army did to known informers.

During the course of 1943, Andrzej Kud was relieved of his duties and Teofil Kielar took his place as sołtyś. As yet another wartime winter set in, Wiktoria Ulma knew that she was pregnant with a seventh child whose birth could be expected in the following spring.

Betrayed

Shortly after midnight on the morning of 24th March 1944, a couple of horse-drawn carts drew up in front of the German police headquarters in Łańcut. Leutnant Dieken, Josef Kokott and two other members of the Green Police, along with four or six members of the Blue Police, one of whom was Włodzimierz Leś, boarded the carts and set off for Markowa. Drawing into the village shortly before dawn, they headed straight for the Ulmas' house. They had been given information and knew exactly where to go and what they'd find. It was almost certainly Leś who had done this. The Szalls had been in contact with him to try to retrieve their property, and although they were careful not to reveal where they were hiding, he'd guessed. The visit to have his portrait taken by Józef had been a ploy to enable him to get into the house to confirm his suspicions. In order not to have to hand back what the Szalls had given him, he'd decided that they should die.

The police entered the house to find everyone sound asleep. Golda and two of the Szall brothers were shot in their beds up in the attic The other Jews were dragged downstairs and outside, and the cart drivers were called by the Germans to come and witness the remaining executions. Edward Nawojski, one of the drivers, would later bear witness to what he heard and saw. Another of the Szall brothers was shot first, then Layka and her child, after them the fourth brother, and finally their father. Next Józef and Wiktoria were stood up outside in front of the house, with their terrified children watching, and shot. Wiktoria began to go into labour as she died. The children were all screaming and crying, and the police briefly conferred among themselves before Dieken gave the order to shoot them too. Kokott, according to Nawojski, personally shot three or four of them. "See how Polish pigs die for concealing Jews," he cried.

Teofil Kielar, the current sołtys, had been sent for but must also have had to be woken up; he arrived just as the last child was killed. Deeply shaken, he asked Dieken why he'd thought it necessary to execute the children as well. Dieken replied cynically that he'd been doing Markowa a favour: it meant that the village wouldn't be saddled with looking after them. Kielar was ordered to collect some men to dig graves, and they set about doing so while the Germans pillaged the house. Among the hastily summoned gravediggers was Franciszek Szylar, who also later bore witness to what had happened. Kokott ordered Szylar to search the bodies of the Jews carefully, and when Szylar found the little box of gold trinkets hidden under Golda's blouse quickly took it off him and pocketed it. The Germans piled up furniture, mattresses and cooking vessels, as well as a large quantity of tanned hides, and demanded that Kielar supply two additional carts with drivers to convey the loot back to Łańcut. Szylar approached one of the Germans to request permission to bury the Ulmas and the Jews separately. Having psyched themselves up to commit the murders, the Germans were in a dangerous mood, and the man reacted with senseless fury, shooting a hole through a bucket Szylar was holding to frighten him into obeying orders without question. Nevertheless, it was agreed that two graves could be made.

Before the police took their departure, in a convoy with carts loaded high, Dieken went to reprimand the Blue Police based in Markowa for their failure to notice that the Ulmas were hiding Jews. The sołtyś was ordered to fetch vodka: he rustled up three litres, and the police finished off their business in Markowa with a drinking spree on the site of the killings. Kokott warned Kielar and the gravediggers to keep their mouths shut about how many people had been shot. On the face of it this was an odd thing to do, because the whole point of executing families that hid Jews was to terrorise the Poles into submission. The explanation is probably that he knew Germany was losing the war. Hitler was still in control of the German war machine, even with his Thousand Year Reich crumbling before his eyes, and still fanatically driving on the process of exterminating Jews and terrorising Poles. His minions dared not wind down the savagery for fear of falling victim themselves, but as they continued to torture and slay, they were all formulating their personal plans to escape retribution.

Constant fear

The Szylar family, who were hiding the Weltzes, lived quite close to the Ulmas, whom they liked and respected. News of what had happened at the Ulma house spread quickly around the village. Eugeniusz was at school when he heard. To avoid exciting suspicion, he had to sit tight, in an agony of fear, till classes ended, before running home to find the house empty. None of his family were there, and he didn't dare check the attic. Towards evening however, when there was no sign of any further trouble, the situation calmed down, with his father, mother, brother and sisters all returning from the other homes in the village where they'd taken refuge. Antoni and Dorota pleaded with the Weltzes to leave and find somewhere else to stay, but they pleaded back, arguing that they had nowhere else to go and that the end of the war was coming closer every day. Antoni said once again – as he'd been saying all along – "God willing, we will survive." Nevertheless, whereas previously the risk they were running had seemed slightly unreal, from that time on the Szylars lived in constant fear.

Yehuda Erlich, a Jew hiding in a nearby village who would survive the war, later testified that immediately after the killing of the Ulmas, other families in Markowa who'd been hiding Jews lost their nerve and killed them themselves. In view of the ruthlessness of the Nazis and the terror under which people were living, the statement was not inherently implausible and was initially accepted. However, Erlich had of course seen nothing for himself: it was hearsay only. If, as he alleged, twenty-four bodies were found in the fields the next day, most people in Markowa would have known about it. The absence of any corroboration whatsoever points to the conclusion that Erlich was mistaken.

When the police looted the Ulmas' home they showed no interest in the books, which were all in Polish and so were left behind. They included the family Bible in which the story of the Good Samaritan had been underlined in red ink. Despite strict instructions not to touch the burial site, five men returned a week later at dead of night, dug up the bodies of the Ulmas and laid them respectfully into coffins before reburying them. Something about this exploit may have reached the ears of the Blue Police or the firefighters, because the next day a patrol was organised around the village. At the Bar household all the family were out working in the fields, and the Riesenbachs were downstairs when they heard dogs barking. Jakub peered out from behind a curtain and saw men approaching the house with guns. The Jews had no time to get into the attic or the cellar, so they all lay down on the floor, near the wall so that they couldn't be seen through the windows. They heard voices at the door, but as nobody appeared to be home the men went away.

The Red Army was on the advance from the east, rolling up the German forces as it came. Most people in Poland would have preferred not to be "liberated" by the Red Army, and those in a position to have a choice made arrangements to get out. Count Alfred Potocki took his departure on 23rd July, heading westwards: he had shipped his personal art collection to Vienna, but had also taken steps to ensure that the castle and grounds would be preserved for the Polish nation. For the many who did not have the choice of leaving, even the Communists had come to look like an improvement compared with the Nazis, at least in the immediate term, and for the remaining Jews their arrival seemed like a miracle because it set them free them from the terrible death sentence under which they'd been living. The Red Army captured Przemyśl on 27th July 1944 and Łańcut on 1st August. On 10th September 1944, Włodzimierz Leś was executed in Łańcut by the Home Army.

Ongoing Trauma and the Suppression of Memories

The bodies of the Ulma family were exhumed and reburied in the village cemetery overlooked by the parish church. However, the post-war situation was extremely fraught. Disorder and violence prevailed for quite some time, with guerrilla warfare between Poles and Ukrainians, and the NKVD busily arresting and torturing suspected anti-Communists. The surviving Jews in Markowa were driven out by a Polish mob, and such was the state of collective insanity that the long-discredited blood libel accusations resurfaced: anti-Jewish riots were incited in Rzeszów and Przemyśl by allegations of the ritual murder of Christian children. The Soviet Union was determined to hang on to what had been eastern Poland, and Poland was compensated by land in the west seized from Germany: the whole country was, as it were, shifted sideways. Any Germans or Ukrainians remaining within the re-drawn borders were expelled. The Iron Curtain then came down with Poland trapped on the Soviet side. For many years thereafter, the true history of the wartime years was suppressed in favour of a false narrative in which the Molotov–Ribbentrop Pact was airbrushed out, the Katyń mass murders blamed on the Germans, the fate of the Jews studiously de-emphasised and the Polish Resistance vilified.

Despite the glaring gaps in what could be investigated, the pursuit of Nazi perpetrators was permissible. Jozef Kokott was captured in Czechoslovakia in 1957 and extradited to Poland to stand trial in Rzeszów. He was found guilty and sentenced to death, but on appeal the sentence was commuted to twenty-five years' imprisonment, and he was never released as he died in 1980. Eilert Dieken had made his way to West Germany, where he sailed through the notoriously lax "denazification" process and was able to continue his police career, eventually being promoted to detective inspector. Only in 1960 were investigations initiated concerning his role in the murder of the Ulmas, and Dieken died that year, thereby escaping human justice.

Research indicates that altogether at least seventeen Jews – possibly twenty-one – survived the war thanks to being hidden by Polish Catholics in Markowa, though they were unable to stay in Poland. The Riesenbachs went to make a new life for themselves in Canada, from where they periodically sent small gifts and sums of money to the Bars. The Weltz family went to the USA. Before they left, they tried to make over some land to the Szylars as a thank-you, but after they'd gone into hiding this land had been allocated to other villagers, and the Szylars decided not to risk incurring resentment by pursuing the matter. They'd not done what they did for a reward. The last few months, however, had been a time of acute stress for all of them, as a result of which Dorota suffered a nervous breakdown. For many years afterwards, the Weltzes kept in touch with the Szylars and sent them parcels. Abraham Segal ended up in Israel.

Righteous among the nations

In 1992, the Szylar family were honoured with the "Righteous among the Nations" award from Yad Vashem, the World Holocaust Remembrance Center, receiving medals bearing the inscription "Whoever saves a single life saves an entire universe". Józef and Wiktoria Ulma were given the award posthumously in 1995: the medals were handed over in Warsaw to Józef's brother Władisław. Recognition of the Bar family came in 1999. In 2004, to mark the sixtieth anniversary of the Ulmas' executions, a large commemorative monument was erected over their grave. Abraham Segal was present for the unveiling and addressed the crowd. In 2016, an Ulma Family Museum was opened in Markowa to tell the story of the Holocaust in Poland and the Poles who rescued Jews. On the day of the opening, an inter-faith service was conducted in the Łańcut Synagogue, and a

ceremony was held in Łańcut Castle to award Polonia Restituta medals (the country's second highest civilian honour) to a long list of rescuers – for the most part posthumously, but including Eugeniusz Szylar and a handful of others still living and present. The Cross of Merit was awarded to Urszula Niemczak, wife of Wiktoria Ulma's nephew, and to Abraham Segal, local politician Bogdan Romaniuk, and researcher Mateusz Szpytma for their hard work in promoting the museum project.

A cause for the beatification of Józef and Wiktoria Ulma and their children, along with other Polish martyrs of World War II, was introduced in 2003. The process for the Ulmas was subsequently separated off from that for the others and entrusted to the Archdiocese of Przemyśl. On 17th December 2022, Józef and Wiktoria, Stasia, Basia, Władziu, Franuś, Antoś, Marysia and the unborn baby were all officially recognised as martyrs, and the date for their beatification was set for 10th September 2023. Fittingly, it was decided that they would be declared "Blessed" in a ceremony conducted by Cardinal Semeraro, Prefect of the Dicastery for the Causes of Saints, among those who treasure their memory, in their own home village of Markowa.

Sources

An invaluable resource in putting together this story was *The Risk of Survival: The Rescue of Jews by the Poles and the Tragic Consequences for the Ulma Family from Markowa* by Mateusz Szpytma, published as a book by the Polish Institute of National Remembrance (IPN) in 2009. I also made use of a very wide range of internet resources, too numerous to list in full, especially Holocaust-related materials collected and made available by Yad Vashem, IPN and other sites. I am particularly grateful for the following items, all accessible online, sharing the stories of three other families:

The Riesenbach family: *https://sites.google.com/riesenbach.com/riesenbach-new/home/riesenbach-family-history/joes-story-of-the-survival-of-the-riesenbach-family*

The Szylar family: *https://ipn.gov.pl/en/news/918,We-couldnt-but-help-them-They-were-our-neighbours-An-Interview-with-Eugeniusz-Sz.html*

The Potocki family: "Alfred Potocki's Role in Helping the Łańcut Community 1939-1944", Jan-Roman Potocki, 2016: *https://old.zamek-lancut.pl/en/content/history/PDF/alfred potocki_eng.pdf*

Image credits

Cover image and pages 4, 22, 25, 53, 63, 64, 78 are from the archive of Mateusz Szpytma.

Pages 16-17: Adobe Stock Images.

Page 29: Everett Collection/Shutterstock.com.

A Prayer for the Intercession of the Ulma Family

Almighty and eternal God,
we thank You for the testimony of the heroic love
of the spouses Józef and Wiktoria with their children,
who gave their lives to save persecuted Jews.

May their prayers and example
support families in Christian life
and help everyone to follow the true path of holiness.

Lord, if it is in accordance with Your will,
kindly grant me the grace…for which
I am asking You through their intercession
and count them among the Blessed.
Through Christ our Lord.

Amen.

Our Father…, Hail Mary…, Glory Be…